3rd

TRITON ELEMENTARY LIBRARY
TRITON SCHOOL CORPORATION
BOURBON, INDIANA

LET'S LOOK AT FARMING

Sylvia Pankhurst

Artist
Carolyn Scrace

Language Consultant
Diana Bentley
University of Reading

The Bookwright Press
New York · 1988

Let's Look At

Castles
Colors
Dinosaurs
Farming
Horses
Outer Space
The Seasons
Sunshine

Library of Congress Cataloging-in-Publication Data

Pankhurst, Sylvia
    Let's look at farming/Sylvia Pankhurst: artist, Carolyn Scrace
      p. cm.
    Bibliography: p.
    Includes index.
    Summary: Discusses various aspects of farming including crops, animals, seasons, and the effects of weather and climate. Also includes a section on fish farming.
    ISBN 0–531–18206–1
    1. Agriculture – Juvenile literature.   [1. Agriculture.   2. Farm life.]   I. Scrace, Carolyn, ill.   II. Title
S519.M54 1988   87–31759
630 – dc19   CIP
                             AC

Phototypeset by Kalligraphics Ltd, Redhill, Surrey
Printed by Casterman S.A., Belgium

First published in the
United States in 1988 by
The Bookwright Press
387 Park Avenue South
New York, NY 10016

First published in 1988 by
Wayland (Publishers) Ltd
61 Western Road, Hove
East Sussex BN3 1JD, England

© Copyright 1988 Wayland (Publishers) Ltd

Words printed in **bold** are explained in the glossary

Contents

The beginning of farming 4
Farming today: crops 6
Farming today: animals 8
Farming today: fish 10
A look at crops around the world 12
Farming and the weather 14
Seasons on the farm 16
Food for farm animals 18
Jobs on the farm 20
Farm buildings 22
Scientists help farming 24
Clearing the land 26
Feeding the world 28

Glossary 30
Books to read 31
Index 32

The beginning of farming

A long time ago people began to farm the land. They caught wild animals and kept them in fields close to their homes. They used them to help with work on the farms or to provide them with food.

Farming long ago

Some people began to grow wheat, barley and other **crops**. At first they used the seed from wild grasses, but later they collected the best seeds from their crops to sow the next year. Slowly the seeds and the crops got better and better.

All over the world, wherever land can be **cultivated**, you will find farms.

Farming today: crops

In the world today there are many different kinds of farms. The crops that farmers grow depend on the weather and the land. In countries that have a very wet, hot **climate** farmers can grow rice, tea, coffee and cocoa.

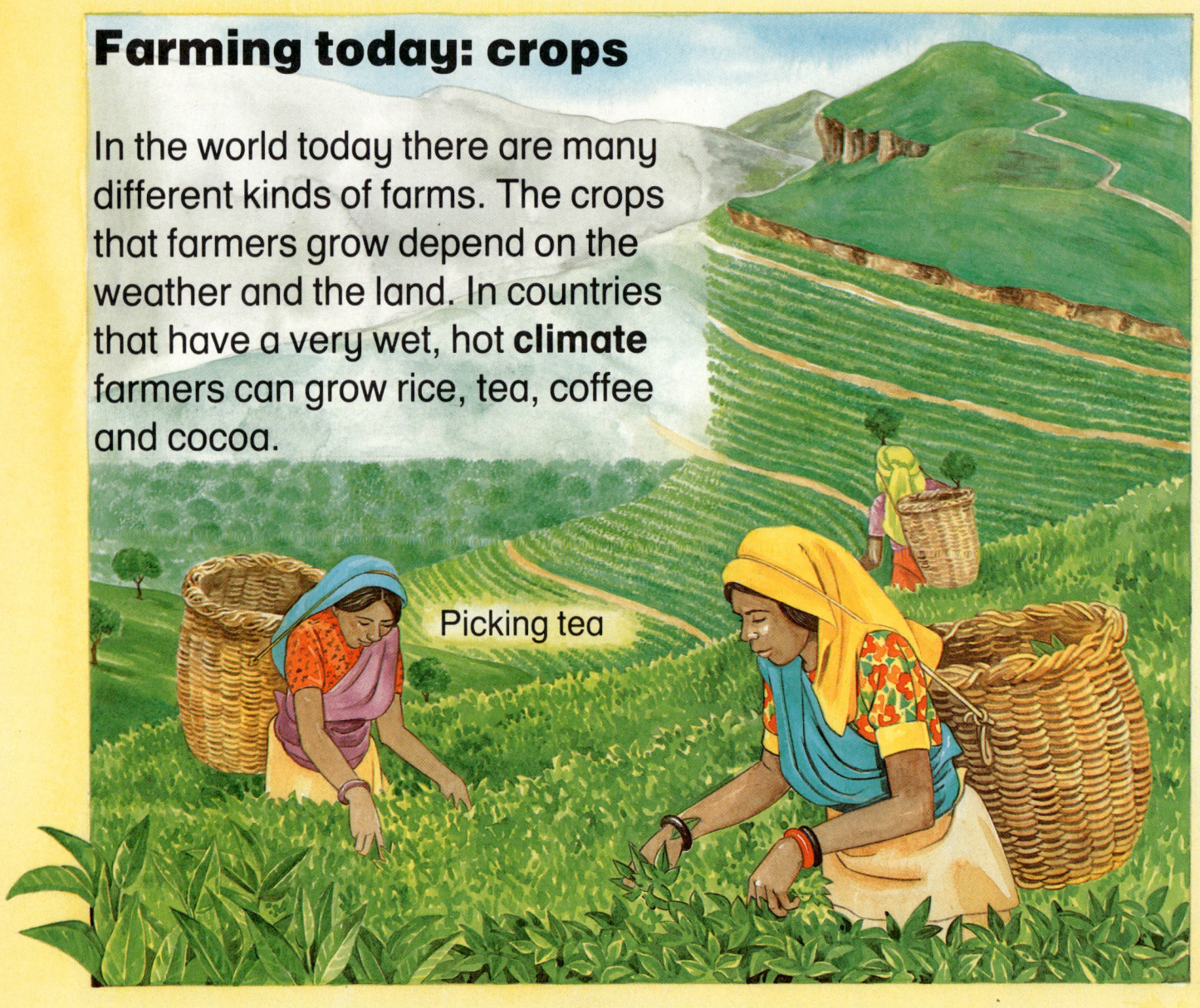

Picking tea

In countries that have a hot, moist climate farmers can grow bananas, oranges, lemons and pineapples.

Growing pineapple

Combine harvesters

In parts of the world where the weather is never very hot or very cold, farmers can grow **cereals** like wheat, barley and oats. Apples, pears and many vegetables also grow well in this climate.

Farming today: animals

Animal farming is also very important. Sheep and goats can be kept in hilly areas. There are more sheep and goats on farms than any other animal. Did you know that there are over 400 million goats in the world?

Like sheep, goats are kept for their milk, meat and hair.

Goats

Merino sheep

Poultry

Hereford bulls

Cattle are also raised all over the world. They are kept mainly for their milk and meat. Some of the milk is used to make butter and cheese.

Did you know that pigs were the first animals to be kept on farms? Pigs provided meat and leather, just as they do today.

Many farmers keep **poultry** such as hens, ducks, turkeys and geese for their eggs and meat.

Pigs

Farming today: fish

Fish is a very important food. People have always caught and eaten fish from lakes, rivers and the ocean. Now fish farmers are **breeding** fish for food, just as they breed farm animals. Fish farming is done in large tanks or in cages that are put in lakes, rivers or the ocean.

A fish farm

Salmon

Trout

Salmon and trout are usually bred in places that are not too hot.

Shellfish such as shrimp and lobster are bred in hot climates. Which would you like to eat?

Lobster

Shrimp

Crops around the world

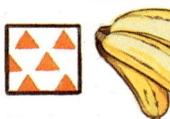

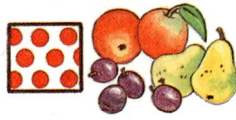

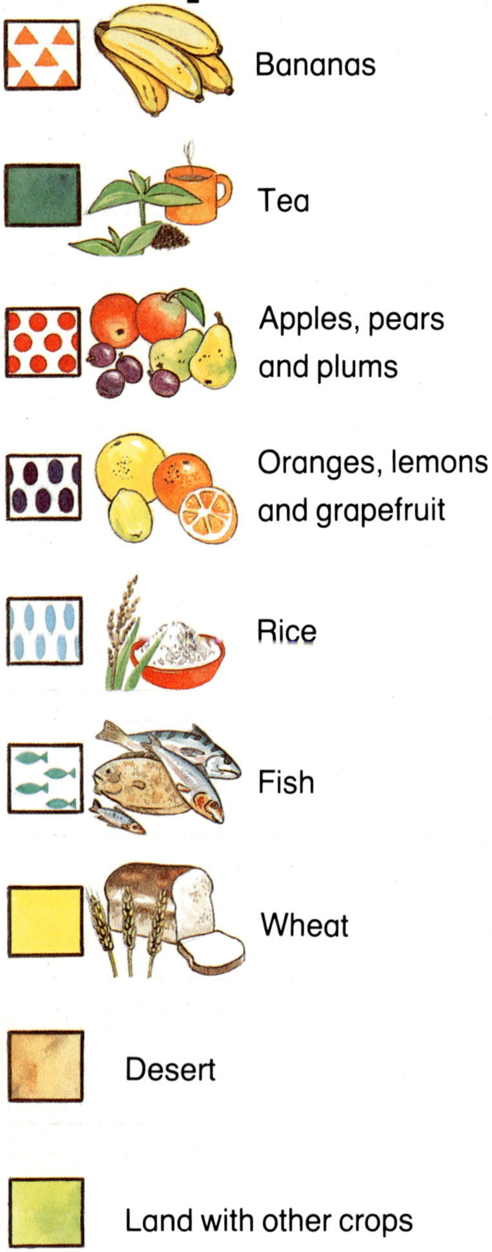
Bananas
Tea
Apples, pears and plums
Oranges, lemons and grapefruit
Rice
Fish
Wheat
Desert
Land with other crops

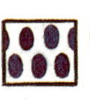

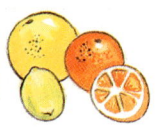

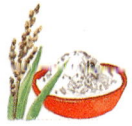

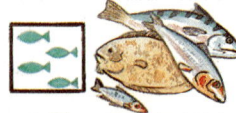

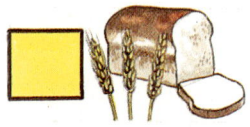

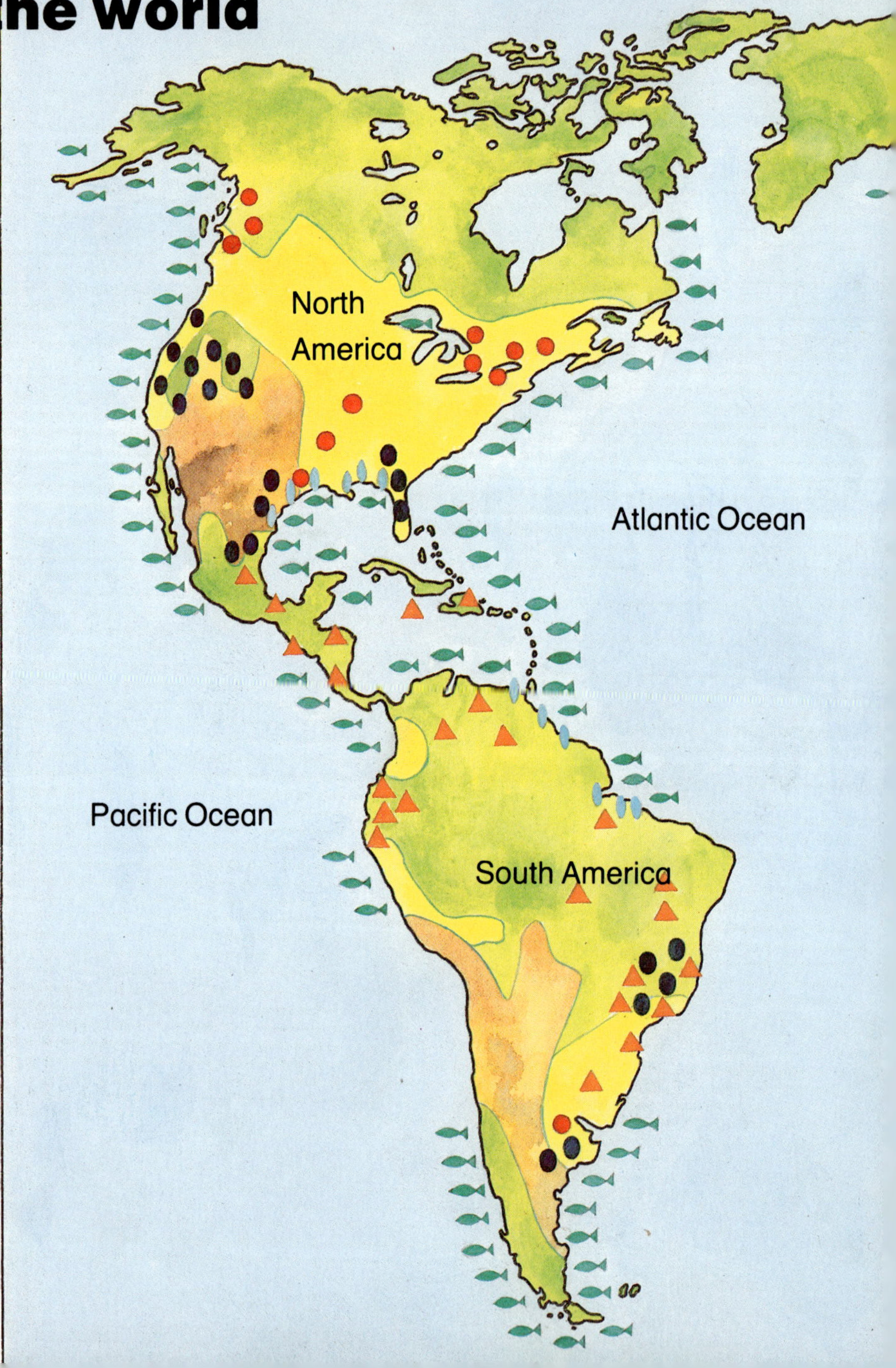
North America
Atlantic Ocean
Pacific Ocean
South America

Farming and the weather

Planting seeds

Farmers are always talking about the weather. Of course it is very important to them. If the seeds are planted too early in the spring, a frost may kill them.

If there is too much rain, the crops may be flooded.

This field of garlic is flooded by rain.

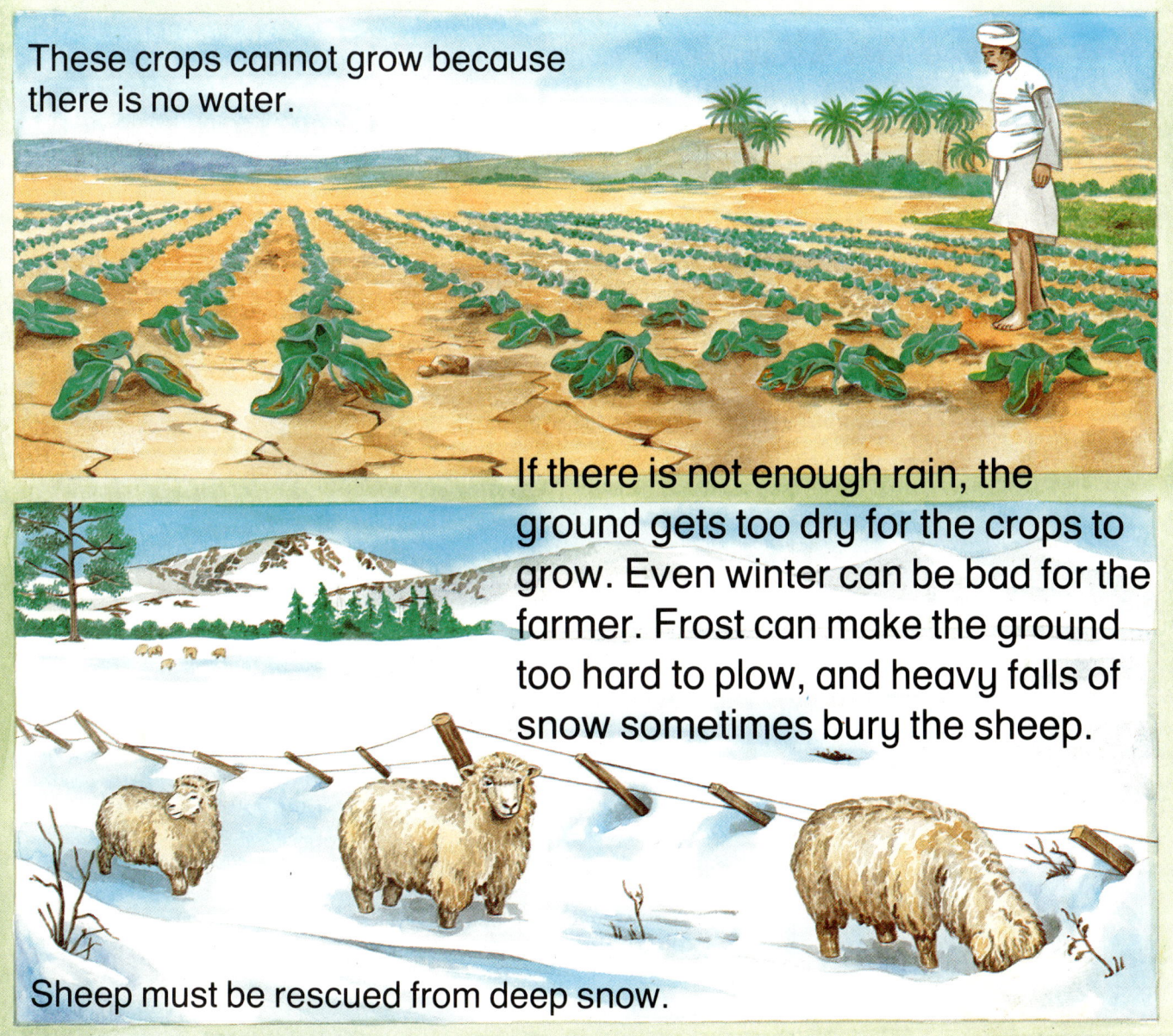

These crops cannot grow because there is no water.

If there is not enough rain, the ground gets too dry for the crops to grow. Even winter can be bad for the farmer. Frost can make the ground too hard to plow, and heavy falls of snow sometimes bury the sheep.

Sheep must be rescued from deep snow.

Seasons on the farm

The work that farmers do depends on the **season** of the year.

In the spring seeds are planted and many animals have their young.

A horse and her foal in the spring.

An airplane sprays crops in the summer to keep them free of weeds and insects.

In the summer, farmers have to keep the crops free of weeds and make sure their animals are healthy.

In the autumn, farmers work very hard. All the crops have to be **harvested** and many of the animals are sent to market.

The farmer brings food for the cattle. He breaks up the ice on the water trough in winter.

Even in the winter, farmers are busy. They have to give extra food to their animals. Machines, fences and walls may need mending. The land is having a rest, but not the farmer!

Food for farm animals

When the weather is warm enough the animals feed outside. They eat grass in the fields or on the hillsides. But in the winter the animals need extra food. Corn or grass is grown and cut in the summer to make into cattle food for the winter.

Cowboys send the cattle off to graze.

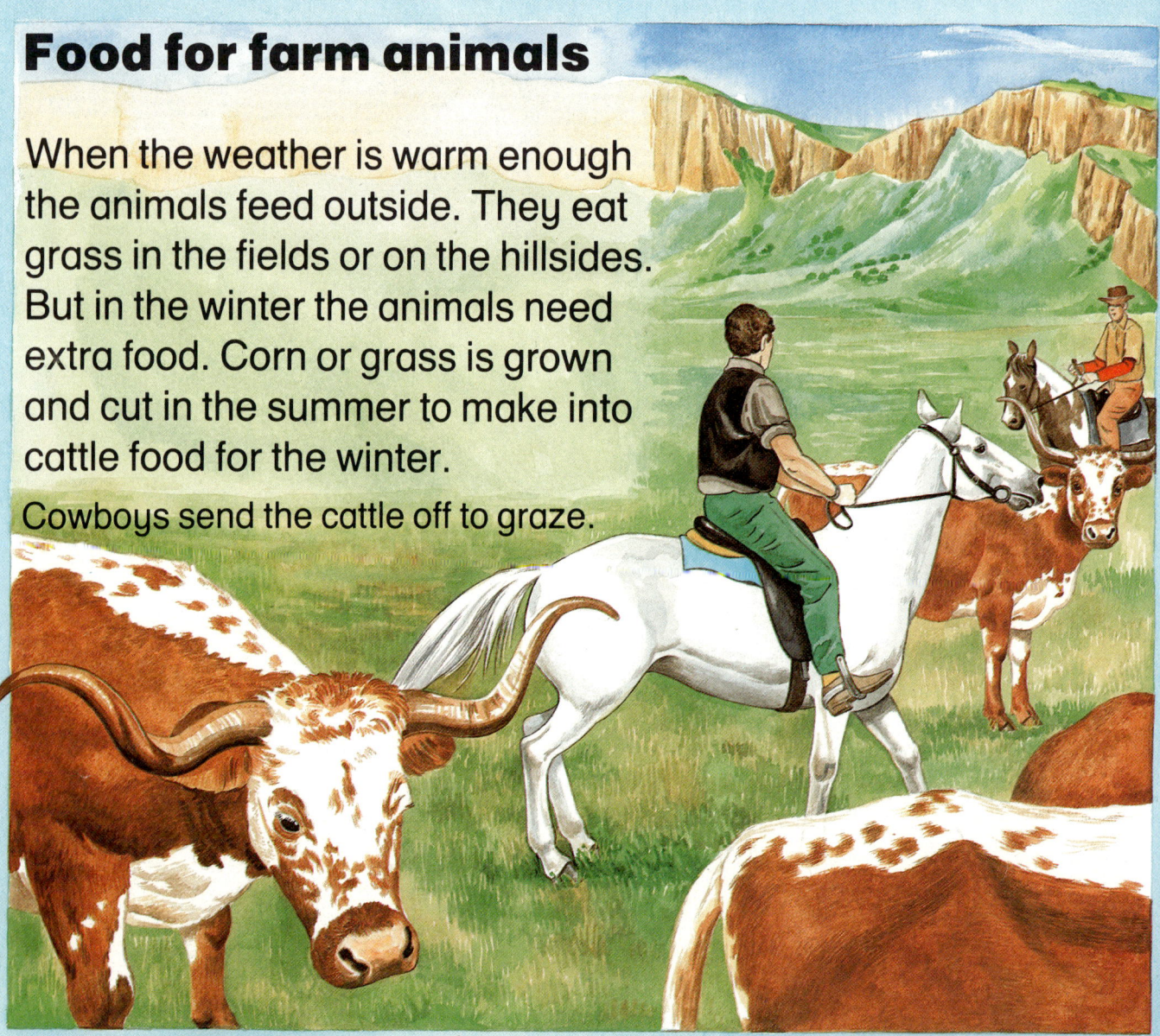

It is stored in barns or big tanks called **silos**. In silos the grass is mixed with **molasses** and smells funny but the animals like it!

The wet cut grass is covered with plastic and stored in a barn.

Jobs on the farm

Farmers have to work very hard and for long hours. They get up very early in the morning. There are many jobs that must be done. Farmers work all day until it is too dark to do any more.

To grow crops and look after animals, farmers have to work hard every day. They have to check and repair their machinery, to make sure it all works well.

Farmers have to take their animals or crops to market.

Farmers have to work out how much things will cost and they have to pay their workers.

At night they like to read farming books and magazines to find out about new ideas.

Farm buildings

Farm buildings are very important. Each building has a purpose. A granary is a place where the farmer stores his grain. A barn is used to store hay. A milking shed is where the cows are milked. A silo is where corn or grass is stored for winter food. A battery is a house where many hens live.

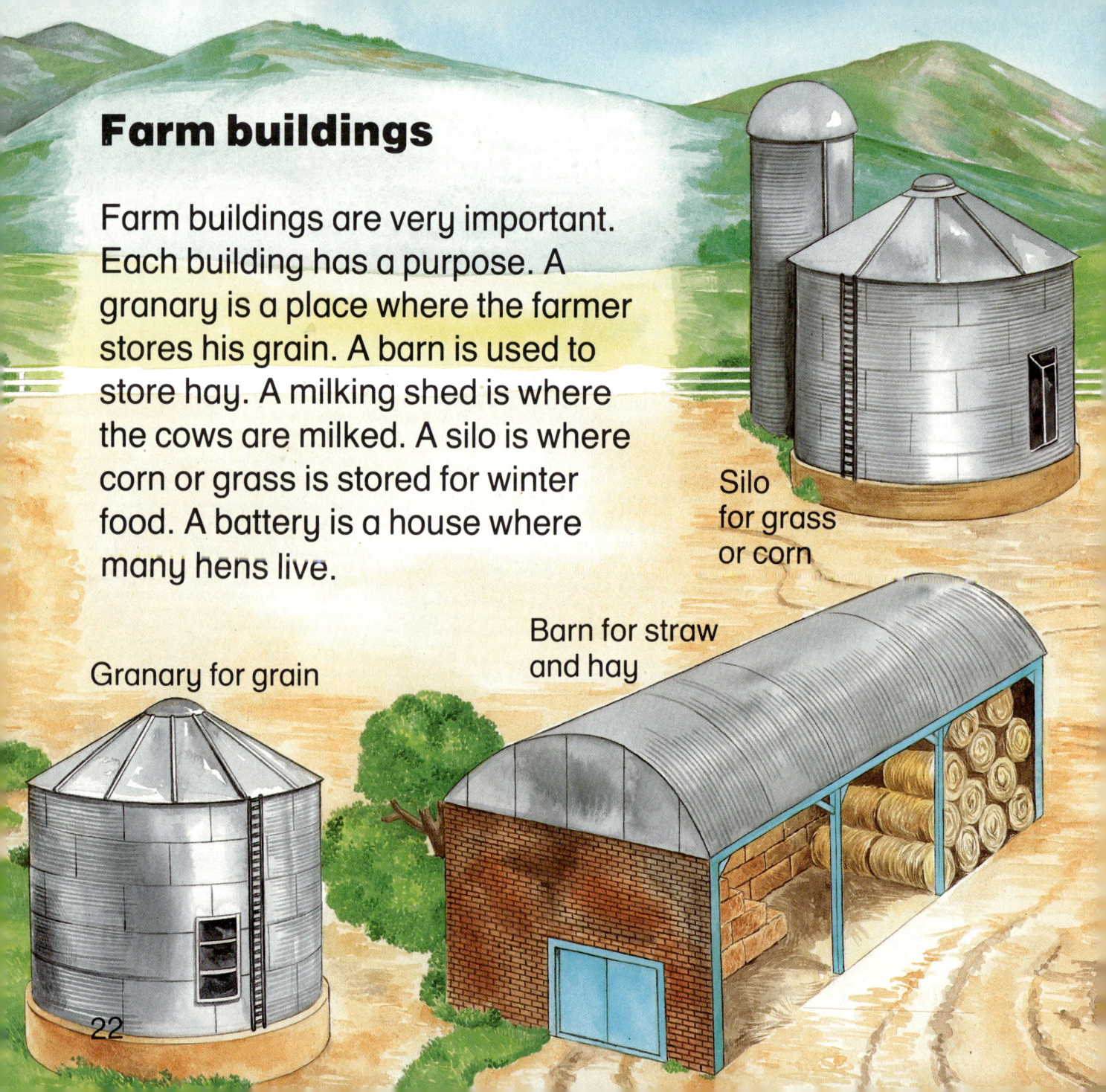

Silo for grass or corn

Granary for grain

Barn for straw and hay

Scientists help farming

Each year there are more and more people living in the world. This means we need more and more food. Scientists have helped the farmer to grow more food. They have discovered ways of improving the soil and controlling the weeds and insects that harm the crops.

The scientist looks at plants to see if they have any diseases.

Clearing the land

In some countries large parts of forests have been cut down to provide land for farms. When people clear away forests it causes many problems. The roots of trees hold down the soil. When trees are cut down, the wind and the weather can wear away the soil.

Chain saw

Anteater

This has turned some parts of the world into desert. Today some people are trying to replant the deserts with trees.

When there are no trees left the soil blows away and leaves desert land.

Feeding the world

An Indian meal

An Australian barbecue

A Moroccan meal

The first farmers had small plots of land and they tried to grow enough food for themselves and their animals. Today farmers around the world grow food to feed people all over the world.

Some farmers in Australia grow food for Europe. Some farmers in the United States grow food for people in Asia. Some farmers in South America grow food for people in the United States. Some African farmers sell food to Australia.

Today farmers in every country help to feed the world.

Glossary

Breeding Raising young ones.
Cattle Bullocks, bulls, heifers and cows.
Cereals Any grain used as food.
Climate Weather conditions.
Crops Plants grown for food.
Cultivate To grow and care for plants.
Disease An illness.
Harvest When the ripe crops are cut or picked.
Molasses A bittersweet syrup left over from sugar.
Poultry Chickens, ducks, turkeys and geese
Seasons Spring, summer, autumn and winter.
Shellfish Water animals that have shells e.g. crabs, lobsters, oysters and scallops.
Silos Big tanks where grass or corn is stored for animal food.

Books to read

All Around the Farm by Alice Low. Random House, 1984.
Ask About Farm Animals Barbara Behn. Raintree Publishers, 1987.
Farm Animals by Tony Jefferis and Judy Hindley. Franklin Watts, 1982.
On the Farm by Eugene Booth. Raintree Publishers, 1985.
Seasons on the Farm by Jane Miller. Prentice Hall, 1986.
The Year at Maple Hill Farm by Alice and Martin Provensen. Macmillan, 1978.

Index

Africa 28
Animal farming
    8–9, 15–16, 18, 28
Asia 28
Australia 28

Barley 5, 7
Barn 22
Battery 22
Breeding 10–11

Cattle 9, 18, 22
Cereals 7
Climate 6, 7, 11
Corn 18–19, 22
Crops 5–6, 14–17, 20–21, 24–5

Cultivation 5

Disease 25

Farmhouses 23
Fish farming 10–11
Fruit farming 6–7

Goats 8
Granary 22
Grass 18–19, 22

Harvest 17
Hay 22

Machines 17, 20
Market 17, 21
Meat 8–9
Milk 9, 22
Molasses 19

Poultry 9, 22

Rice 6

Scientists 24
Seasons 15–18, 22
Seeds 5, 14, 16
Sheep 8, 15
Silos 19, 22
Soil 26–7
South America 28

Vegetable farming
    7, 12–17, 25

Weather 6–7, 14, 18, 26
Weeds 16, 24
Wheat 5, 7

#1791   3rd   95193

630   Pankhurst, Sylvia
Pan
      Farming

TRITON ELEMENTARY LIBRARY
TRITON SCHOOL CORPORATION
BOURBON, INDIANA

 GUMDROP BOOKS - Bethany, Missouri